SCHIRMER PERFORMANCE EDITIONS

SCHUMANN

SELECTIONS FROM ALBUM FOR THE YOUNG

Opus 68

Edited and Recorded by Jennifer Linn

To access companion recorded performances online, visit:
www.halleonard.com/mylibrary

Enter Code
8172-6481-2593-0435

On the cover:
Home, Sweet Home
by George Dunlop Leslie
(1860-1920)

© Fine Art Photographic Library/CORBIS

ISBN 978-0-634-09875-8

G. SCHIRMER, *Inc.*

DISTRIBUTED BY
HAL•LEONARD®
CORPORATION

7777 W. BLUEMOUND RD. P.O. BOX 13819 MILWAUKEE, WI 53213

www.musicsalesclassical.com
www.halleonard.com

CONTENTS

HISTORICAL NOTES

SCHUMANN AND THE MUSICAL HOME

*W*hat would I not do for love of you, my own Clara!" Even though Robert Schumann (1810-1856) composed all the pieces in this *Album*, he could not have done so without the inspiration of his wife, Clara Wieck Schumann. Their pairing remains one of the most famous in music history, and the family they raised—they had eight children together—inspired the *Album for the Young.*

The two met while Robert was a piano student of Clara's father, the renowned pedagogue Frederich Wieck. One of the elite students invited to board at the Wieck household, Schumann met his future wife when she was only nine years old. Though a master teacher, Wieck focused most of his energy on the talents of his extraordinary daughter; she blossomed into a concert pianist and toured throughout Europe. Over the years, Clara and Robert's friendship deepened to love, but Clara's domineering father turned cruel in his attempts to prevent a marriage between the two, even disinheriting his daughter. After years of acrimony that ended famously in a lawsuit, the couple was granted legal permission to marry and finalized their union in September, 1840.

By the time of his marriage, Schumann had already enjoyed a varied and successful musical career. Initially he had hoped to be a concert pianist—even his future father-in-law recognized his potential as a virtuoso—but his hands were injured as a result of using a mechanical finger-strengthening device. He then focused his efforts on composing, as well as editing the music journal *Neue Zeitschrift für Musik* (New Music Journal). These two activities brought out his gifts with language, for even as an adolescent, Schumann had fancied himself more a poet than a musician. His *lieder,* of course, constitute one of his great legacies, but written language also

infused his daily activities, from vigilantly maintaining a house diary and writing copious letters to friends and colleagues, to creating touchingly poetic love letters to his beloved Clara.

The household they created centered almost entirely around music and their children. At a time when men often distanced themselves from the daily rigors of parent-ing, Schumann was an involved father who part-icipated in his children's play and education. Inspired by his home life, which helped provide him with a mental stability that he struggled all his life to maintain, Schumann wrote a great deal of *Hausmusik*: modest, everyday music to be practiced and performed in the home. In addition to the works written for the adult amateur (e.g., Op. 70, 73, 74), Schumann composed several playful sets for children. According to Clara, these sets grew from the games Schumann watched his children play. They include the evocative *Waldszenen* (Forest Scenes), with a mysterious world befitting a child's storybook, and the *Song Album for the Young*, with poetry by Goethe and Schiller, among others. Still, his first foray into *Hausmusik*, the *Album for the Young,* Op. 68, remains his most admired, even to this day.

Upon composing the *Album*, Schumann recognized that the literature for beginning pianists was scant and uninspiring, so he created musically interesting pieces specifically with children's interests, emotions, size, strength, and abilities in mind. Ultimately this remains the innovation in the *Album for the Young* that has been copied for more than a century since.

—*Denise Pilmer Taylor*

Clara Schumann and daughter Marie, for whom the *Album for the Young* was composed.

Daguerrotype, 1844 or 1845
Courtesy of Robert-Schumann-Haus Zwickau;
Archiv-Nr.: 12336 - B2

Title page, first edition. Illustrations by Ludwig Richter. Clockwise from bottom left:
33. *"Weinlesezeit — fröhliche Zeit!"* 13. *Erster Verlust* 10. *Fröhlicher Landmann*
22. *Rundgesesang* 15. *Frühlingsgesang* 24. *Ernteliedchen* 35. *Mignon*
12. *Knecht Ruprecht* 8. *Wilder Reiter* 38 & 39. *Winterszeit I & II*

Courtesy of: **Robert-Schumann-Haus Zwickau**; Archiv-Nr.: 4501, Bd. 10 - D1/A4

PERFORMANCE NOTES

Robert Schumann composed the *Album für die Jugend (Album for the Young)*, Op. 68 in 1848 with such a creative vigor that it seemed to defy the tumultuous events that had occurred just months before its conception. Fanny Mendelssohn, a friend of Robert and his wife Clara, died in May of 1847. Later that summer, their eldest son Emil died tragically, followed by Felix Mendelssohn (their dear friend and godfather to their daughter Marie), who passed away suddenly in November. Along with their personal tragedies, the Schumanns endured the anxiety of political revolutions that were sweeping across Europe. Despite this turmoil, the master of the miniature found renewed inspiration in his desire to create new piano pieces for his daughter Marie. In a letter to Carl Reinecke in October 1848 Schumann reports:

> I wrote the first pieces for the Album specifically for the birthday of our oldest child, and then more pieces came to me one after another; it was as if I were once again starting to compose from the very beginning. You will also detect something of my earlier humor.[1]

For her seventh birthday on September 1st, Robert composed six pieces (Op. 68 no. 2-7) included in the *Geburtstagalbum für Marie* (Birthday Album for Marie). By the end of September, in a fury of creative energy, he completed the remaining pieces of the Album, 43 in all. Schumann's desire to compose pieces for children (rather than simply reminiscent of them, as in the *Kinderscenen*) grew from his distaste for the mindless keyboard drills commonly used in the teaching of his day. Clara Schumann commented:

> ...the pieces children usually study in piano lessons are so poor that it occurred to Robert to compose and publish a volume (a kind of album) consisting entirely of children's pieces. Already he has written a number of attractive miniatures.[2]

Although Robert had stepped down from his role as editor of his highly acclaimed journal *Neue Zeitschrift für Musik* only a few years earlier, it is clear that he still had a desire to continue his mission to educate the public.

Robert Schumann's talent for infusing imagination and beauty into even the smallest forms had already set him apart as a composer, but his interest in combining pedagogical content with an aesthetic nature that children could embrace was something rare indeed. The *Album for the Young* was first published in 1849, and since then it has continued to be a model collection, forever influencing keyboard pedagogy and captivating hearts, young and old, with its vivid imagination and musical poetry.

The Individual Pieces

This edition contains the following 15 selections from the *Album for the Young,* Op. 68.

Melodie (Melody)

If musicianship is the primary focus of Schumann's intended new approach to keyboard pedagogy, then a beautifully shaped melody is a perfect beginning and perhaps the single most critical skill to be achieved. Therefore, it is no surprise that Schumann begins his Album with "Melody." It is interesting to note the expressive markings over single notes in mm. 5-7 and 13-15. These can be realized only with flexible timing (agogic accent), supporting Schumann's ongoing desire to step away from the metronomic pulse of common finger drills of the day into a more thoughtful and expressive way of playing.

Soldatenmarsch (Soldiers' March)

In contrast to the *legato* phrasing and expressive flexibility of "Melody," "Soldiers' March" is detached, strict, and unwavering. At the time this march was composed, the sound of parading soldiers was surely a familiar one due to the many uprisings in Europe. The dotted rhythms found throughout support the military character of this solo. The curious *forte* markings placed on each downbeat in mm. 1, 5, 9, 13, and 17, (and purposefully absent in others) clearly direct the performer to avoid playing the dotted rhythm as an upbeat. The result is a piece with crisp character and timeless wit. Schumann was able to capture in sound the image of a child marching like the most serious soldier (perhaps with a less than perfect gait?), bringing a tongue-in-cheek smile to any listener's face.

Trällerliedchen (Humming Song)

In the *Geburtstagalbum für Marie* (the "birthday" album Robert gave Marie for her seventh birthday), this piece was originally titled "Little Slumber Song for Ludwig." The dedication to Schumann's infant son Ludwig brings to light the innocent spirit of this gentle piece. As in "Melody," Schumann begins this piece with a beautifully shaped melody in the right hand and an eighth-note accompaniment in the left hand. However, in the second section, the right hand must now play *both* the melody and the accompaniment, calling upon the thumb notes to be voiced gently—a technique commonly required in Schumann's later piano works. "Humming Song" is a perfect introduction to this concept.

Stückchen (Little Piece)

"Little Piece" revisits the friendly key of C Major previously introduced in "Melody" and "Humming Song." A right-hand melody with eighth-note accompaniment appears once again, but this time with a twist. Here, the melody begins on beat three rather than the downbeat. This up-beat phrasing continues with three "question" phrases that keep the line spinning forward over shifting harmonies until it finally comes to rest on the Tonic (mm. 8 and 16). In mm. 12-14, the curious change in slurring, the sole *crescendo - diminuendo*, and the change in harmony (note the L.H. C♯), all suggest an expressive *rubato*. In the *Geburtstagalbum für Marie* one finds the added instruction, "to be played after schoolwork is finished." Schumann writes in the *Erinnerungsbuchelchen* (journal): "Yesterday (September 21, 1847) was the big day when she, [Marie] lap-desk under her arm, first wandered into the school for reading and writing."[3]

Jägerliedchen (Hunting Song)

With this rollicking piece, complete with the sounds of horn calls and horses' hooves, Schumann introduces the key of F Major and 6/8 meter. In the original manuscript, Schumann does indicate the damper pedal for mm. 1-2, 5-6, 9-10, and 13-14, adding to the imagery of the horns echoing through the countryside. Contrasting *legato* and *staccato* touches, lively accents (especially the right-hand accent in m. 25), and sudden dynamic changes all provide new challenges for the developing pianist.

Wilder Reiter (Wild Rider)

Certainly one of the more famous pieces from the entire Album, "Wild Rider" continues the 6/8 meter and *staccato* touch of the previous "Hunting Song." Mindful perhaps of the need for strengthening left-hand technique, Schumann gives the melody to the left hand in the B section. After hearing the melody played with the stronger right hand in the beginning, the student will naturally want to play it equally well with the left hand. "Wild Rider" begins in A minor and, although the B section revisits F Major (from "Hunting Song"), the left-hand melody avoids accidentals, using only the white keys, thus keeping the piece accessible yet challenging.

Fröhlicher Landmann (The Merry Farmer)

"The Merry Farmer" is one of the most treasured pieces in the student repertoire, and is aptly characterized by Clara Schumann, "...first the father sings alone; in the second part his little boy chimes in."[4] Ludwig Richter's drawing for the first edition charmingly illustrates this scene (see page 34).

Continuing to focus on the left hand, Schumann begins this happy melody in the bass, with lightly-bouncing accompaniment chords in the right hand. Then, both hands play the melody in tandem, signaling a joyous end to the father and son's shared workday.

Sicilianisch (Sicilienne)

This festive peasant dance begins in 6/8 meter with an upbeat; both the meter and single upbeat are characteristics of this dance form, which originates in Sicily. The 6/8 meter that was first introduced in "Hunting Song" and "Wild Rider" is reinforced here. The descriptive tempo marking *schalkhaft* (which literally means "roguish"), gives a slightly different character to the generally graceful *sicilienne* often danced at weddings and celebrations. In the contrasting section (mm. 26-37), the surprising meter shift to 2/4, along with the addition of lively sixteenths, help to create a sudden, mischievous mood, reminiscent of the character Florestan, found in the mature works of Schumann. Students can be encouraged to create their own imaginative story line to bring to life the interesting contrast between the seemingly unrelated musical ideas in this piece.

Kleine Studie (Little Study)

In an earlier draft of the Album, Schumann had included his arrangements of familiar tunes composed by legendary German masters including Bach, Beethoven, Handel, Gluck, Haydn, Mozart, and Mendelssohn. Schumann originally wanted to give students an historical perspective with these arrangements, and he had a particular affinity for Bach that is evident in the style of "Little Study," which was included in the final version. The obvious parallel to the "C Major Prelude" from J.S. Bach's *Well-Tempered Clavier* is but one example of Schumann's ability to recreate various composers' styles expertly. An excellent study in *legato* playing, this piece requires an even touch and finesse in shaping musical lines to achieve the subtlety and nuance necessary for a truly musical performance.

Erster Verlust (First Loss)

The vignette suggested by the illustration created by Ludwig Richter for this piece (see p. 35) portrays a young girl sadly mourning her little bird lying dead by an open cage. Perhaps this sorrow was inspired by an actual event: Schumann's daughter Eugenie reported that in the January before her father had written the Album he had fed marrow-balls to their little greenfinch, who certainly enjoyed the tasty morsels, but died unexpectedly shortly thereafter. One can certainly understand the sudden burst of anger (articulated by the accented chords in mm. 29-30), given these circumstances! The *fp* that occurs on the first note, and again on the last eighth note in m. 8, implies a slight "lingering" before rushing on to the downbeat, giving the player time to allow the note to decay sufficiently before continuing. The sighing two-note slurs throughout add to the poetic despair and invite even the young pianist to express the sense of tragedy keenly in this brief, poignant solo.

Schnitterliedchen (The Reaper's Song)

The drone of the *musette* (a French bagpipe) in the left hand and the grace notes reminiscent of a bagpiper's embellishments in the right hand give this piece its rustic charm. Schumann returns to the key of C Major and to 6/8 meter, skillfully reinforcing previous concepts. Mindful also of equal development of the hands, Schumann writes the *legato* melody in mm. 13-20 for both hands in octave unison (as in "The Merry Farmer"), requiring careful attention to fingering, especially in the left hand. The technique of executing the grace notes with the precarious fourth finger while dutifully holding down the sustained note with the thumb (mm. 1-2) can be managed more readily by observing Schumann's helpful tempo marking *Nicht sehr schnell* (not very fast). A passage in double notes in the right hand in m. 29 is also challenging, but is thoughtfully written with a slightly easier *staccato* touch, showing Schumann's awareness

of a child's technical limitations. A similar instance appears in "The Merry Farmer" (m. 10 and m. 16), where Schumann indicates *portato* touch for the right-hand descending double notes.

Kleine Romanze (Little Romance)

The *Album for the Young* was originally divided into two parts: *Für Kleinere* (For Littler Ones) and *Für Erwachsenere* (For More Grown-up Ones). "Little Romance" is the first piece in the second part and is one of the few selections from the Album in which Schumann clearly indicates a metronome marking in the manuscript. At first glance, the tempo indication *Nicht schnell* (not fast) and the seemingly quick metronome marking (♩=130) do not seem to agree, but the restless and unpredictable nature of "more grown-up ones" along with the emotional surges in the music (i.e. the *crescendo* to *fp* and *diminuendo* in mm. 1-2) lend support to Robert Schumann's original metronome marking. In "Little Romance," as in the "The Merry Farmer," Schumann writes the melody in unison octaves between the hands (a duet between lovers perhaps?) but with added, guitar-like accompaniment chords.

Reiterstück (The Horseman)

This stunning miniature could be characterized as a "Wild Rider" for the "More Grown-up Ones." "The Horseman" begins with an upbeat in 6/8 meter and is written in a minor key, just as the earlier "Wild Rider." The vivid sound images created by the galloping cadence of the broken octaves, challenging rhythms, distinct articulations, bold accents, and sweeping dynamics all come together to create an exhilarating sensation as the horseman approaches from afar, arrives triumphantly, and then vanishes on the horizon. In his manuscript, Schumann clearly indicates his ideal tempo with the metronome marking ♩=100. Particularly challenging for the developing pianist is the extended *diminuendo—nach und nach schwächer* (gradually more faint)—as the horseman fades from sight. Students will find an excellent technical bonus in this piece—practicing wrist rotation.

★ ★ ★ (No. 30)

We do not have a direct explanation from Robert Schumann regarding the enigmatic trio of stars written above three of his pieces from the Album: Nos. 21, 26, and 30; however, when his daughter Eugenie asked Clara about them, she replied: "Perhaps your father wanted the stars to reflect parents' thoughts about their children."[5] It is interesting to note that in the original manuscript the images are hand-written as asterisks, but in the first published edition they appear as five-pointed stars.

Number 30 is one of the lesser-known pieces in the entire Album. Its introspective nature and relatively moderate technical demands in a slower tempo make it a perfect piece for the returning adult student or reticent teen. The < > markings that first appeared in "Melody" are also found here in mm. 10 and 12, making this an effective piece in which to teach *rubato*.

The opening motive is restated several times throughout this piece, giving the student experience expressing the same idea in many subtle ways. With no title assigned to it by Schumann, the student can use his imagination to create a personal, expressive interpretation for this piece.

Mignon

Mignon is a character in *Wilhelm Meister*, a novel by one of Schumann's favorite authors, Wolfgang von Goethe. In the story, a troupe of traveling gypsies comes to town and Mignon appears as a mesmerizing child beauty and acrobat, entertaining the crowds with her precarious tightrope dance. Schumann originally titled this piece "Tightrope Girl" in his manuscript, but he later crossed it out and changed it to "Mignon." Richter's title- page illustration aptly portrays the original title (see page 35).

Schumann ingeniously recreates a delicate tightrope walk in musical language with the walking descent of the dotted half notes in the left hand, set against a right-hand melody that lingers on the fourth-beat *fp*'s in mm. 1-4, thus evoking the image of a slightly rocking "Tightrope Girl." The drama continues in mm. 14-16 with *sf* on the climactic note of the soaring melody. Even the tactile sense of the fingers balancing on the black-key flats adds to the musical realization of the exquisitely delicate character, Mignon.

In m. 7 there is some controversy regarding the first right-hand note. In the manuscript it is without a doubt B♭, but in the first printed edition, in which Robert (not Clara) oversaw the corrections, it is an A♭; however, the proofs are lost. In this edition we have chosen to use A♭ in the score, with the option of substituting B♭ as indicated at the bottom of the page.

Fingerings

In the first publication of the *Album for the Young*, Schumann indicated fingerings only sparsely on "Melody" and a few other pieces not included in this edition. All fingerings in this book are those of the editor.

Tempo and Metronome Markings

All tempo indications are as they originally appeared in the edition published by Schuberth & Co. in 1849. The only metronome markings Schumann wrote for the selections in this edition are found in "Little Romance" and "The Horseman." Musicologists and pianists have long debated Schumann's metronome and its questionable worthiness, as well as the differences in taste between Robert and Clara. I tend to agree with Clara's comment, made as she was working on the 1887 edition of her husband's works, that determining metronome marks was "pure torment." After comparing the tempos of recorded performances by several noted contemporary pianists with Schumann's markings and the metronome markings of Clara Schumann's edition (which are at times somewhat unbelievable), I came to the conclusion that less is more and so have not suggested metronome settings or ranges for any of the pieces. The words and instructions left by the composer in his score and in general, throughout his writings on music, should suffice in choosing tempos that accommodate and conform to the performer's technical ability and musical taste, as well as what is considered stylistically appropriate.

Pedal Markings

All pedal markings are placed in the music as they were notated in the original edition; however, we have opted to use modern *legato* pedal symbols ⌞∧⌟ in place of the antiquated 𝓟𝓮𝓭. and ✳ symbols. Any editorial pedal suggestions are shown by a dotted line.

Musical Rules for Home and Life

In the original edition of the *Album for the Young,* Schumann included an additional section entitled *Musikalische Haus und Lebensregeln* (Musical Rules for Home and Life). We have translated them and have included them in this edition on pages 36-39.

These rules—68 brief aphorisms in all—include practical and often humorous advice for the developing musician regarding practicing, listening, and selecting appropriate repertoire, as well as ideas for achieving the loftier goals of spirit and artistic purity.

Rule No. 68 says it best:

> *Es ift des Lernens kein Ende —*
> *"Learning has no end."*

—*Jennifer Linn*

References

Appel, Bernhard. "'Actually Taken Directly From Family Life': Robert Schumann's *Album für die Jugend.*" Translated by John Michael Cooper, in *Schumann and His World.* Edited by R. Larry Todd. Princeton: Princeton University Press, 1994.

Appel, Bernhard R. Robert Schumann's *"Album für die Jugend" Einfuhrung und Kommentar.* Zurich und Mainz: Atlantis Musikbuch-Verlag, 1998.

Deahl, Lora. "Robert Schumann's *Album for the Young* and the Coming of Age of Nineteenth-Century Piano Pedagogy." *College Music Symposium* vol. 41, 2001.

Otswald, Peter. *Schumann: The Inner Voices of a Musical Genius.* Boston: Northeastern University Press, 1985.

Schumann, Eugenie. *Erinnerungen.* Stuttgart: J. Engelhorns Nachf., 1927.

Facsimile of the original manuscript used in this edition:
Robert Schumann. *Jugend-Album Opus 68.* Robert-Schumann-Haus, Zwickau, Germany. hg. v. Georg Eismann, Leipzig: Peters 1956

A special note of thanks to Dr. Gerd Nauhaus, Direktor Forschungs- und Gedenkstätte, Robert-Schumann-Haus Zwickau, Germany

Photos courtesy of Robert-Schumann-Haus, Zwickau, Germany

Notes

1. Quoted in Bernhard Appel, "'Actually Taken Directly From Family Life': Robert Schumann's *Album für die Jugend,*" trans. John Michael Cooper, in *Schumann and His World,* ed. R. Larry Todd (Princeton: Princeton University Press, 1994), 182
2. *Ibid.,* 171
3. *Ibid.,* 183
4. Eugenie Schumann, *Erinnerungen,* (Stuttgart, J. Engelhorns, 1927), 167
5. *Ibid.,* 168

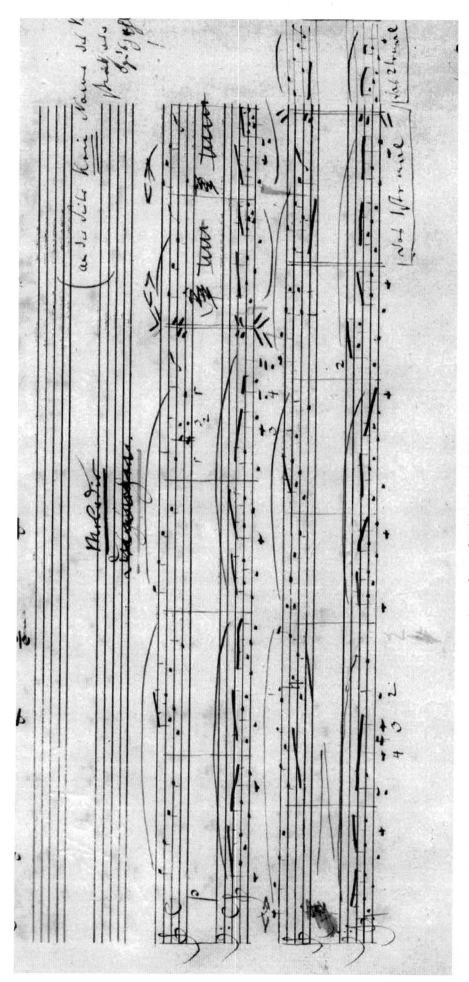

Autograph copy of "Melodie," from the *Album for the Young.*
Courtesy of: **Robert-Schumann-Haus Zwickau**; Archiv-Nr: 10955 - A1

Melodie
Melody

Robert Schumann
Op. 68, No. 1

Soldatenmarsch
Soldiers' March

Robert Schumann
Op. 68, No. 2

Munter und straff
Lively and strict

Trällerliedchen
Humming Song

Robert Schumann
Op. 68, No. 3

Stückchen
Little Piece

Robert Schumann
Op. 68, No. 5

Jägerliedchen
Hunting Song

Robert Schumann
Op. 68, No. 7

Frisch und fröhlich
Briskly and merrily

Wilder Reiter
Wild Rider

Robert Schumann
Op. 68, No. 8

Fröhlicher Landmann,
ven der Arbeit zurückkehrend
The Merry Farmer, Returning from Work

Robert Schumann
Op. 68, No. 10

Sicilianisch
Sicilienne

Robert Schumann
Op. 68, No. 11

Schluß
Fine

Schnell
Fast

Vom Anfang ohne Wiederholungen bis Schluß
From the beginning to Fine without repeat

Kleine Studie
Little Study

Robert Schumann
Op. 68, No. 14

Leise und sehr egal zu spielen
Lightly and very evenly

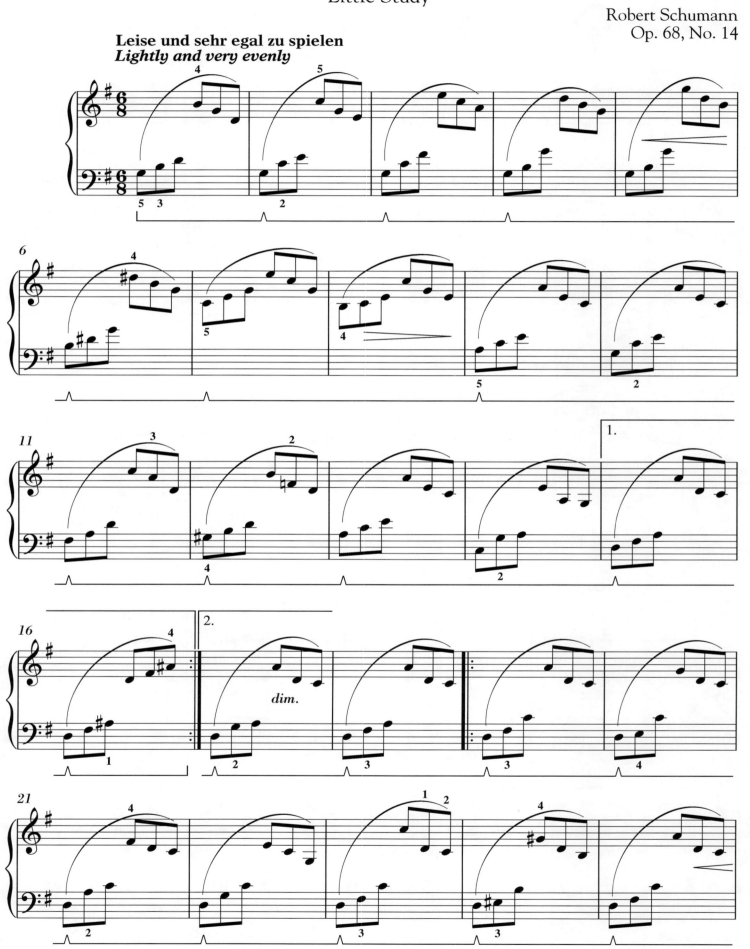

*ossia

Erster Verlust
First Loss

Robert Schumann
Op. 68, No. 16

Nicht schnell
Not fast

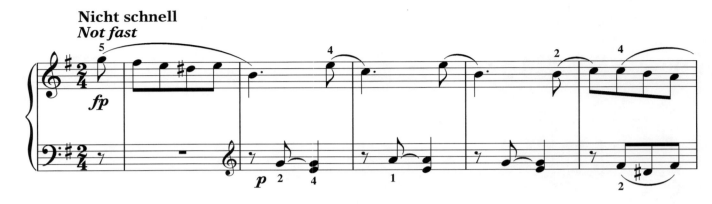

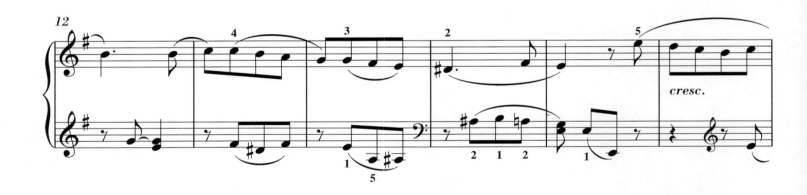

etwas langsamer
somewhat slower

im tempo
in tempo

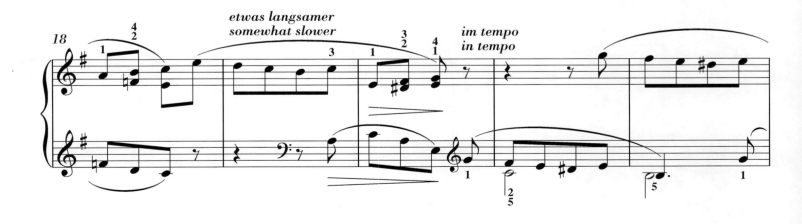

Schnitterliedchen
The Reaper's Song

Robert Schumann
Op. 68, No. 18

Kleine Romanze
Little Romance

Robert Schumann
Op. 68, No. 19

Reiterstück
The Horseman

Robert Schumann
Op. 68, No. 23

Robert Schumann
Op. 68, No. 30

Sehr langsam
Very slowly

Mignon

Robert Schumann
Op. 68, No. 35

* The first note in m. 7 is a B♭ in the original manuscript. However, in the first printing which was supervised by
Robert, the note is altered to A♭. (Courtesy of Dr. Gerd Nauhaus, Director of The Robert-Schumann-Haus Zwickau.)

The Merry Farmer

Wild Rider

The illustrations on pages 34 and 35 by Ludwig Richter are details taken from
the title page of the first edition of the *Album for the Young.* The full title page is reproduced on page 4.

Mignon

First Loss

MUSICAL RULES FOR HOME AND LIFE

1. Development of hearing is most important. Strive early on to identify music and sounds. The bell, the pane of glass, the cuckoo—research which pitches they produce.

2. You should practice scales and other finger exercises diligently. There are, however, many people who intend to accomplish everything through these, continuing many hours of daily mechanical practice into their old age. This is like someone striving every day to say his ABCs faster and faster. Make better use of time.

3. Someone has invented the so-called "silent keyboard." Try one for a time in order to see that they are suited for nothing. One cannot learn to speak from a mute.

4. Play in time! The playing of many virtuosi is like the path of an intoxicated person. Don't take them as a model.

5. Learn the fundamental rules of harmony early.

6. Don't be afraid of the words "theory," "general bass," "counterpoint," etc.; they will come to you as friends when you do the same to them.

7. Never jangle the keys. Always play freshly and never play a piece halfway.

8. Dragging and rushing are equally great mistakes.

9. Strive to play light pieces well and beautifully; it is better than weighty, mediocre repetitions.

10. Always play on a well-tuned instrument.

11. You should not only be able to play your little pieces with your fingers, you must also be able to hum them without the piano. Sharpen your imagination this way, so that you are able to commit to memory not only the melody of a composition, but also the harmony.

12. Try, even if you have only a small singing voice, to sing from the music without the help of an instrument. This will improve the sharpness of your hearing. If you have a full-sounding voice, don't hesitate a moment to develop it. Think of it as the most beautiful gift the heavens lent you.

13. You must reach the point that you understand music on paper.

14. When you play, don't concern yourself with who hears you.

15. Always play as if a master is listening.

16. When someone sets a composition in front of you for the first time so that you should play it, look it over first.

17. If you have done your musical work for the day and feel tired, then don't exert yourself through more work. It is better to rest than to work without desire and freshness.

18. As you become older, play nothing that is fashionable. Time is precious. One would need one hundred lifetimes to learn just the finest things.

19. One does not grow to be a healthy person on sweets, pastry, and candy. Like food for the body, food for the mind must also be nourishing and hearty. The masters provide sufficiently for the latter. Pay attention to them.

20. All passage work changes with the times. Only when talent serves a higher purpose does it have worth.

21. You do not have to circulate bad compositions. On the contrary, help suppress them with all your strength.

22. You are neither to play nor listen to bad compositions, if you are not forced to.

23. Never strive for so-called *bravado* execution. Seek the expression the composer intended. Doing more than that creates a distorted image.

24. Regard it as something horrible to change or omit something, or add modern ornaments in pieces by good composers. This is the biggest disgrace you can inflict upon art.

25. With regard to selection of the pieces you study, ask your elders; you will save much time this way.

26. You must always continue to learn the important works of the important masters.

27. Abandon the applause that great virtuosos so often receive. The applause of artists is worth more than that of the masses.

28. All pieces that are fashionable will become unfashionable again. If you practice these in your old age, you will become a pompous fool, which no one respects.

29. Much playing in social gatherings is more harmful than useful. Consider the public, but never play something you will have to be ashamed of later.

30. Miss no opportunity to make music with others, in duos, trios, etc. It makes your playing purposeful and animated. Also, accompany singers often.

31. If everyone wanted to play first violin, we would have no orchestras. Therefore, respect each musician in his place.

32. Love your instrument. However, do not in vanity regard it as the greatest and only one. Bear in mind that there are others just as beautiful. Bear in mind also that there are singers that give music its greatest utterance.

33. When you get older, associate more with scores than with virtuosos.

34. Play the fugues of the great masters industriously, most of all those of Johann Sebastian Bach. The *Well-Tempered Clavier* is your daily bread. Then you will certainly become a proficient musician.

35. Select among your friends those who know more than you do.

36. Relax from your industrious musical studies by reading poetry. Go outdoors often.

37. Let yourself learn a great deal from singers, but don't believe them in everything.

38. People live on the other side of the mountain as well. Be modest! You have not invented or thought up anything that others have not already discovered or created. And if you have, regard it as a gift from above that you have to share with others.

39. The study of music history, supported by listening to masterpieces from the different eras, will quickly cure you of conceit and vanity.

40. A beautiful book on music is *Über Reinheit der Tonkunst* (Purity in Music) by [Anton Friedrich Justus] Thibaut. Read it often as you grow older.

41. If you pass a church and hear an organ playing inside, go in and listen. If you are allowed to sit on the organ bench, try to play with your little finger and be astonished at the force of the music.

42. Miss no opportunity to practice on the organ; there is no other instrument that takes such revenge on careless or messy passage playing.

43. Make a point to sing in choirs, particularly the inner voices. This makes you more musical.

44. But what does "musical" mean? You are not it if you play your piece laboriously to the end with your eyes fixed fearfully to the notes; you are not it if, when someone turns two of your pages at once, you get stuck and cannot go on. But you are it if you know what is coming in a new piece as though you know it by heart already; in a word, if you have music not just in your fingers, but also in your head and heart.

45. But how does one become musical? Dear Child, the main things, a sharp ear and quick technique, as with all things, come from above. But this talent can be shaped and increased. You become it [musical] not by the fact that you lock yourself in seclusion all day long performing mechanical studies, but by participating in many various musical interactions, in particular by working a lot with choir and orchestra.

46. Get to know the four main types of the human voice early on. Listen to them particularly in the chorus. Explore in which range their greatest strength lies and in which other range they can be used for a gentle, tender sound.

47. Listen studiously to all folk songs, as they are a storehouse of the most beautiful melodies and reveal glimpses of the character of the various nations.

48. Practice early reading the old clefs. Otherwise many treasures of the past will remain locked to you.

49. Pay attention early on to the sound and character of the various instruments; seek to stamp their characteristic tone quality in your ear.

50. Never miss hearing good operas.

51. Honor the old, but also turn to the new with a warm heart. Look to unknown names without prejudice.

52. Don't pass judgment on a composition after one hearing; that which pleases you at first is not always the best. Masters want to be studied. Many will become clear to you only in your old age.

53. When forming an opinion on compositions, determine if they belong in the category of art or are intended for the amusement of amateurs. Partake of the first type—don't be bothered by the others.

54. Melody is the battle cry of amateurs, and certainly music without melody is not music at all. But understand what that means: only the easily understood, rhythmically pleasing have worth. There is also another type and when you look up Bach, Mozart, and Beethoven, you see a thousand different melodies. Hopefully you will quickly become tired of the poor, new Italian opera melodies in particular.

55. Look for short melodies to play together on the piano, that are perhaps pretty; but if they come to you spontaneously, not at the piano, that should make you even happier because the spirit of music moves within you. The fingers must do what the head wants, not the other way around.

56. If you catch on to composition, then make up everything in your head. Try rehearsing a piece with instruments only when you have it completely finished. If your music came from within, with feeling, then it will affect others in the same way too.

57. If the heavens gave you an active imagination, you will often sit spellbound for hours at the piano, wanting to express your soul in harmony, and feel pulled into secret, magic circles, even if perhaps the realm of harmony is unclear to you. These are the happiest hours of youth. Nonetheless, be careful, you have been given an additional talent that tempts you to waste strength and time on shadows. You can only gain control of this way of working by constantly writing it down. Therefore, write more when you improvise.

58. Get to know conducting early and watch good conductors often; even conduct in silence. This will develop clarity in you.

59. Look around thoroughly in life, and also in the other arts and other subjects.

60. The rules of morality are the same as the rules of life.

61. Through diligence and perseverance you will bring yourself ever higher.

62. From a pound of iron, which costs a few cents, let yourself make many thousand watch springs, which are worth in the hundred-thousands. Use the pound God has given you conscientiously.

63. Without enthusiasm, nothing real can be accomplished in art.

64. Art is not there to make you rich. Become an ever greater artist; all other things will come to you from within yourself.

65. Only when the form is completely clear will the essence become clear.

66. Perhaps only the genius can fully understand genius.

67. It has been said that a consummate musician must be capable, on the first hearing of a complicated orchestral work, of seeing the actual score before him. This is the highest thinking one can achieve.

68. There is no end to learning.

—Translated by Elaine Schmidt

ABOUT THE EDITOR

JENNIFER LINN

An accomplished pianist, teacher, and clinician, Jennifer Linn is a contributing composer and arranger for the *Hal Leonard Student Piano Library*. Her editions and recordings for the G. Schirmer Performance Editions include *Clementi Sonatinas*, Op. 36 and *Schumann Selections from Album for the Young*, Op. 68. She is also co-editor of the HLSPL Technique Classics books *Hanon for the Developing Pianist* and *Czerny: Selections from the Little Pianist*, Opus 823.

Ms. Linn has presented recitals, workshops, and master classes throughout the United States and Canada, appearing at the World Piano Pedagogy Conference, Music Teachers National Association national conventions, and MTNA state programs throughout the United States. Because of her expertise as a pianist and composer, Ms. Linn frequently judges both piano performance and composition events throughout the country. Her own students have competed successfully in state and national competitions, and her original compositions have been selected for the National Federation of Music Clubs' festival list and have been featured in *Keys* magazine. She is a member of the Missouri Music Teachers Association and has taught piano privately for over twenty years.

Ms. Linn has held the position of Visiting Lecturer in Piano Pedagogy at the University of Illinois at Urbana-Champaign and has been a faculty member of the Illinois Summer Youth Music Piano Camp since 1998. She is a member of Who's Who of American Women as well as Who's Who in America. Ms. Linn received her B.M. and M.M. in Piano Performance from the University of Missouri-Kansas City (UMKC) Conservatory of Music where she was the winner of the Concerto-Aria Competition. She was also awarded the prestigious Vice Chancellor's Award for Academic Excellence and Service.